21 DAYS
TO SEXUAL PURITY

A Biblical Devotional For
Overcoming Sexual Temptations

DEON O. THOMAS

ISBN: 1499259344
ISBN 13: 9781499259346

This book is dedicated to Dr. Roy and Mrs. Sadie Thomas. I can never thank both of them enough for providing me with such godly and Christ-centered training. You both have not been merely parents, but the very tools that the Lord has seen fit to use to help me conform more and more into the image and likeness of Jesus Christ.

TABLE OF CONTENTS

Introduction · vii
Day 1   Our God Is Savior · 2
Day 2   Do You Love Me? · 8
Day 3   The Choice Is Mine · 12
Day 4   No More Excuses · 16
Day 5   My Daily Bread · 20
Day 6   I will train My Mind · 24
Day 7   God's Word…My Weapon · · · · · · · · · · · · · · · 28
Day 8   Watch Your Eyes · 34
Day 9   Run For Your Life! · 38
Day 10   Tell It Like It Is · 42
Day 11   It's Time To Pray · 46
Day 12   Our God Forgives · 52
Day 13   God's Will Revealed · 56
Day 14   Are We On The Same Page? · · · · · · · · · · · · · · 62
Day 15   The Blessed Man · 66
Day 16   Don't Blame God · 70
Day 17   I Don't Want My Desires · · · · · · · · · · · · · · · · 74
Day 18   Watch Your Words! · 78

Day 19   Fearing God · 82
Day 20   It's Time To Add · 86
Day 21   It's All About Him · 90
Epilogue · 95

INTRODUCTION

This devotional has been written to help you walk in sexual purity. It has been divided into 21 brief chapters and each has been specifically designed to accomplish just one task that will help you to overcome sexually impure tendencies. Although you could probably read through this devotional in a single sitting, I would definitely hasten to advise you not to do so. Instead of racing to finish it enjoy the journey. Read only one chapter a day and allow the word of God to speak to you and change you as you meditate on each day of the journey.

There are a couple of features that have been put into each day to help you receive the maximum benefit from this life changing devotional:

1. Each chapter begins with a verse or a couple of verses. Don't gloss over them; read them slowly and prayerfully and allow the Lord to change you through them.

2. For each day there is a thought which relates directly to the verses given. Take your time and make sure you understand what is being said. Re-read the thought for the day and underline those areas that stand out to you.

3. At the end of each thought is a short statement for you to remember. This helps to summarize the thought for the day into one sentence or phrase.

4. Each day there is a specific challenge designed to help you live victoriously and walk in a sexually pure manner. Do the challenges, don't skip them. They are specifically designed to provide you with a necessary practical step that will empower you to walk in sexual purity.

5. Finally, each chapter has a closing prayer that is designed to do two things: Firstly, it helps those who do not know how to pray to learn to pray and secondly, it helps to give a template from which you can start off praying and proceed into your own prayer.

The journey to sexual purity is one that is filled with many failures but the journey is worth it. My prayer for you is that as you work through this devotional and put into practice the challenges for each day, you will experience the power of the living God, the beauty of holiness and be filled with an insatiable desire to please the Lord and walk before Him in holiness.

Let us begin our journey!

OUR GOD IS SAVIOR

"Our God is a God who saves; from the Sovereign Lord comes escape from death"

Psalm 68:20

"She will give birth to a son, and you are to give him the name Jesus, because he will save his people from their sins".

Mathew 1:21

Sexual purity is tough business. For most of us, (if not all of us) we have struggled to control our sexual desires at one point or another. Let me be quick to say that our sex drive is a God-given gift. We were created by God and our sexual urges were definitely a part of His creation. The Lord doesn't expect us to somehow get rid of these desires. He definitely wants them expressed but he has provided a context in which we can be truly free to express them and that context is marriage. The problem for most of us, however tends to fall into one of two categories;

1. We have powerful sexual urges and are not yet married OR

2. We are married but still finding it hard to control our urges.

Whatever the situation, sexual purity is possible with the help of the Lord. Fortunately, we have not been left to ourselves to keep ourselves sexually pure; quite frankly, we can do no such thing. The Lord is the one who gives us the strength to walk before him in sexual purity and we receive this strength by first understanding His character.

On this first day of our journey there is one very important thing we ought to know about God and that is, He is a God who saves (Psalm 68:20). He is not a God who condemns, or hates or despises us. He is a mighty savior and his desire for each and every one of us is that we would experience his saving power in every aspect of our lives.

Some people think that the Lord is more eager to destroy than to save, but such thinking is totally contrary to what the Bible teaches. When God sees wickedness, His first move is to save us from destruction by calling us to repentance. The story of Jonah beautifully demonstrates this point. Jonah was a prophet who was sent by God to preach against the great but wicked city called Nineveh. He didn't want to go at first but let's just say that he eventually changed his mind through a series of divine interventions. When he went to Nineveh and preached the word of God the people of that city repented of their sins and turned from their wickedness. One would have expected Jonah to have been pleased with the mighty revival that occurred, but Jonah was very angry. He apparently wanted God to destroy them for their wickedness instead of giving them an opportunity to repent (Jonah 4:1). Jonah learned that God's first move is never to destroy because He is gracious, compassionate, slow to anger, abounding in love and He is one who relents from sending calamity (Jonah 4:2).

Although God hates all sin (Hebrews 1:9) He has demonstrated His deep desire to save us from our sins through the birth of Jesus Christ. The word of God says: "For God so loved the world that he gave his one and only Son, that whosoever believes in him shall not perish but have eternal life" (St. John 3:16). Jesus is God incarnate and the reason for his birth, death on a cross and resurrection was to save mankind from their sins. The Lord does not want our sins to rule over us, enslave us or destroy us. He wants us to be delivered and saved from our sins. Jesus is the only person who can save us from the power and the penalty of sin and we can experience his mighty saving power if we renounce and repent of our sins and accept Him as the Lord of our lives.

Accepting Jesus as Lord is the first and most important step towards walking in purity. When Jesus has first place in our hearts everything else will submit to Him. It is only through Him that we can experience true freedom from our sins.

Remember:

God saves.

Challenge:

Memorize Psalm 68:20.

"Our God is a God who saves; from the Sovereign Lord comes escape from death."

Psalm 68:20

Prayer For Today

Heavenly Father, I praise you because of who you are. I praise you for being so gracious, compassionate, slow to anger and abounding in love towards me. Repeatedly you have demonstrated to me that you are a great Savior and I thank you for saving me from being destroyed by my sins. Thank you for demonstrating your great love to me by sending your Son Jesus Christ into this world to die on a cross for my sins. Father, I repent of my sins and ask you to forgive me of all my sins, cleanse me from all unrighteousness and save me from all impurity, especially sexual impurity. Teach me your ways, fill me with your Holy Spirit and saturate my being with an insatiable desire for your word. I thank you for life and life abundantly. In Jesus' name I pray.

Amen.

PERSONAL REFLECTIONS

DO YOU LOVE ME?

"Love the Lord your God with all your heart and with all your soul and with all your strength."

Deuteronomy 6:5

Imagine for a moment that you are standing before a store filled with sexually immoral material and Jesus approaches you and asks "Do you truly love me more that these?" ('These' could be anything. It could be sexual immorality, pornography, lustful thoughts or any other sin). Besides feeling totally embarrassed, how would you respond? Remember, this is no ordinary person asking you this question. This is Jesus, God in the flesh who knows your deepest thoughts and desires. He knows everything about you; He knows your weaknesses and your strengths. He even knows what you would be thinking at the point you are being asked this serious question.

At possibly the lowest point in Peter's life, Jesus approached him and asked him this same question. After seeing my own failures, I possibly would have responded by saying: "I want to love You, Lord" or "I'm trying to love You, Lord". Although Peter was an apostle who understood from personal experience what it meant to fail the Lord, he responded by telling the Lord that he loved him. It wasn't that Peter was a hypocrite, no, not at all. Peter was definitely bothered by his failures just as any other person who has come into the saving knowledge of Jesus would be, but Peter also knew how to turn to the Lord. When the Lord came to Peter, Peter showed his love for the Lord by going to Him. He did not choose to remain in his guilt, shame or sin; instead he turned away from all the negative emotions that overwhelmed him and turned to the Lord.

When we fail the Lord, our God approaches us and provides us with an opportunity to turn to Him. One powerful sign that we love the Lord is seen in our willingness to turn away from our failures and turn to the Lord. Peter could have exalted his failures above the power of the Lord to forgive and restore but instead he turned away from his failures and approached the Lord. Peter showed his love by walking in the "R" word, that is, he REPENTED.

In the same way that the Lord approached Peter in his time of failure, so the Lord will approach us by the Holy Spirit and the question directed at Peter is the same one that we must answer. "Do you truly love me more than these?". Let us respond to the Lord like Peter. Let us turn from our guilt, our shame and our sin and turn to the Lord and say: "Yes, Lord, I love You more".

Remember:

Keep turning to the Lord.

Challenge:

Memorize Deuteronomy 6:5.

"Love the Lord your God with all your heart and with all your soul and with all your strength."

Deuteronomy 6:5

Prayer For Today

Heavenly Father, I turn to you today. I turn away from wallowing in guilt and shame and sin and I turn to You, my Lord and savior. Father, forgive me for exalting my failures over your power to forgive and restore me. Today, I repent of my sins and I ask you to wash me in your precious blood. Cleanse me from the stain of my sins and fill me with a deep and passionate love for you. Give me the strength today to walk in the love I have for you and to turn away from that which displeases you. In Jesus' name I pray.

Amen.

PERSONAL REFLECTIONS

THE CHOICE IS MINE

"Love the Lord your God with all your heart and with all your soul and with all your strength."

Deuteronomy 6:5

"This day I call heaven and earth as witnesses against you that I have set before you life and death, blessings and curses. Now choose life, so that you and your children may live"

Deuteronomy 30:19

"For by him all things were created: things in heaven and on earth, visible and invisible, whether thrones or powers or rulers or authorities; all things were created by him and for him."

Colossians 1:16

Everything in this world was created by God and for God (Colossians 1:16). The beauty about the Lord is that although He created us, He has given us the choice to offer ourselves to Him. No matter what situation we find ourselves we have the

God- given power to decide what we will do. We can't necessarily control what the outcome of our choices will be but we definitely have the ability to choose what we will do irrespective of the situations in which we are placed.

God wants us as His creation to choose Him out of our own volition; He certainly will not force us. In Deuteronomy 30:19 the word of God says: "This day I call heaven and earth as witnesses against you that I have set before you life and death, blessings and curses. Now choose life, so that you and your children may live". This powerful verse shows us that the Lord has given us an opportunity to choose and he instructs us as to what choice we should make. He says to us: "choose life".

Each and every day options are set before us and we must daily choose the option that will produce life. Some choices can destroy us and our posterity while others will produce life to ourselves and to those around us. Whenever we are given the opportunity to make a choice, it is important that we at least ask ourselves if life will be produced or death.

Sexual sin only produces death. There is absolutely not one ounce of life in it. It shatters relationships, it degrades our bodies, it tarnishes our reputation and destroys trust. As we aim to walk in sexual purity, we must practice to choose life over death. Every time we face the temptation to be sexually immoral or impure, we must remember that our Lord and Savior has given us the power to choose. Let us choose life over death today.

Remember:

You always have a choice.

Challenge:

Memorize Deuteronomy 30:19.

"This day I call heaven and earth as witnesses against you that I have set before you life and death, blessings and curses. Now choose life, so that you and your children may live".

Deuteronomy 30:19

Prayer For Today

Heavenly Father, I thank you for this day. Thank you for creating me and giving me the power to choose. Strengthen my inner man and help me today to choose life over death. As I hide Your word in my heart, I pray that You will give me the victory over sexual sin. Father, I surrender my sexual desires to You and ask you to fill me with Your precious Holy Spirit and help me to bring glory to Your name in all my actions today. All these things I pray, in the name of Jesus.

Amen.

PERSONAL REFLECTIONS

NO MORE EXCUSES

"No temptation has seized you except what is common to man. And God is faithful; he will not let you be tempted beyond what you can bear. But when you are tempted, he will also provide a way out so that you can stand up under it."

1 Corinthians 10:13

There are some people who are excellent at making excuses. If they are late, it is somebody else's fault. If they can't get a job, it is because of the 'system'. If their pay is not the best, it is the government's fault. Some excuse their behavior by putting the blame on their upbringing, their social status, their family history or their friends, while others even go as far as blaming God.

Unfortunately, many people carry this blame game into their spiritual walk as well. When some individuals sin against the Lord they find someone or something on which to pin the blame, instead of taking responsibility for their actions. While it might be easier to blame others for our own spiritual failures, we will never be able to stand in the day of temptation if we do not practice to take responsibility for our actions.

In every temptation to sin sexually we must keep in mind three specific thoughts. These three thoughts come directly from 1 Corinthians 10:13.

1. God is faithful.

2. God will not allow us to be tempted beyond what we can bear.

3. God will provide a way out of every temptation we face.

God is Faithful
When the Bible says that God is faithful, it means that he is trust-worthy. This means that what He says, He does. One verse that unequivocally speaks to the faithfulness of the Lord is found in Hebrews 13:8 which states: "Jesus Christ is the same yesterday and today and forever".

God will not allow us to be tempted beyond what we can bear
Because the Lord is faithful, we can rest assured that He will see to it that we are never tempted in a manner that we cannot bear. Satan is that one who tempts us to do evil and he will always try to make us feel as if we have to fail the Lord. But we must stand on what the word of God says and resist the temptation to accept and believe the lies of the devil. If our God says we can handle it, then that's it. No matter how powerful the temptation seems, let us remember that the Lord is saying that through Christ we have the spiritual fortitude to stand against that temptation. We do **not** have to give in to it.

God will provide a way out of every temptation we face
The third and final thought to bear in mind is that, in every tempta-tion, God in his faithfulness will provide a way out for us. In every temptation we must ask the Lord to **show** us the way out. There is always a way out. Sometimes the way out might be as simple as running away or speaking out; at other times, it might be to con-fess to someone that we are feeling tempted or it might mean that we have to call on the name of the living God. Whatever the way, we can rest assured that God will provide us with an opportunity to get out and away from every temptation.

Let us stand today and resist the temptation to do evil by remembering that we serve a faithful God who is always helping us to walk in victory.

Remember:

You have the spiritual strength through Christ to resist temptation.

Challenge:

Memorize 1 Corinthians 10:13.

"No temptation has seized you except what is common to man. And God is faithful; he will not let you be tempted beyond what you can bear. But when you are tempted, he will also provide a way out so that you can stand up under it."

1 Corinthians 10:13

Prayer For Today

Heavenly Father, I am so thankful that You are a faithful God. Thank You for giving me the spiritual strength to withstand every temptation that could ever come my way. I also thank You Lord for providing a way out of every temptation that I will face today. Strengthen my inner being and help me today to believe Your word above all the lies of the enemy. All these things I pray in the name of Jesus.

Amen.

PERSONAL REFLECTIONS

MY DAILY BREAD

"Do not conform any longer to the pattern of this world, but be transformed by the renewing of your mind. Then you will be able to test and approve what God's will is- his good, pleasing and perfect will."

Romans 12:2

"They are not just idle words for you - they are your life."

Deuteronomy 32:47a

Every spiritual battle first has its origins in the mind. On a daily basis we experience temptations on varying levels. We face the temptation to look at an individual and lust, or we are tempted to feast our eyes on pornography or we are tempted to read sexually explicit material or sometimes we are tempted to just go out and indulge in casual sex. What all these temptations have in common is that they start with thoughts in our minds. The enemy is always trying to fill our minds with his sinful suggestions. He wants us to think on his immoral thoughts so that we can start having the feeling to sin. The 'feeling' to sin comes after we have the thought about sin.

To many Christians, it is hard to conquer these immoral thoughts. Although our enemy would love us to think that no solution exists for these impure thoughts, the truth is we can successfully tear down these thoughts with one powerful spiritual weapon that has been provided for us. That weapon is the word of God. The Bible must be read and re-read if we are ever going to win the battle in our minds and in our lives. Psalm 119:9 says: "How can a young man keep his way pure? By living according to your word". This lifestyle of living according to the word of God is what is absolutely necessary for one to live a life of purity. We can only live according to God's word if we first *know* the word of God.

Each day, we have to make it our commitment to spend time reading the Bible. Let us not be ignorant of the word of God. Let us fill our minds with God's word and allow the Spirit of God to empower us to stand in the day of temptation.

Remember:

God's word is not an idle word it is your life (Deuteronomy 32:47a).

Challenge:

1) Memorize Romans 12:2.

"Do not conform any longer to the pattern of this world, but be transformed by the renewing of your mind. Then you will be able to test and approve what God's will is- his good, pleasing and perfect will."

Romans 12:2

2) Make a commitment to read at least three chapters from the Bible each day. If you miss a day or didn't have the time to get through three chapters in a day, don't worry about it, just get back up and keep going. By reading three to four chapters from the word of God each day you will read through the whole bible once in a year. Remember as the word of God comes into your life you will grow stronger and stronger and be better able to stand against temptations.

Prayer For Today

Heavenly Father, I thank You for Your powerful word. Thank You for filling me with power as I read Your word and meditate on it. As I spend time in Your word Lord, I ask You to open my eyes and cause me to see wonderful things. Create in me a never-ending desire for Your word and help me to be faithful to obey Your word in the different tests and temptations I will face today. All these things I pray in Jesus' name.

Amen.

PERSONAL REFLECTIONS

I WILL TRAIN MY MIND

"Those who live according to the sinful nature have their minds set on what that nature desires; but those who live in accordance with the Spirit have their minds set on what the Spirit desires".
Romans 8:5

"Finally brothers, whatever is true, whatever is noble, whatever is right, whatever is pure, whatever is lovely, whatever is admirable- if anything is excellent or praiseworthy- think about such things."
Philippians 4:8

"Rather, clothe yourselves with the Lord Jesus Christ, and do not think about how to gratify the desires of the sinful nature."
Romans 13:14

Although the whole Bible has greatly impacted my life, there are certain verses that have made an indelible impression on my mind. One such verse says: "Have nothing to do with god-less myths and old wives' tales; rather, train yourself to be godly" (1Timothy 4:7). This verse teaches us that we do not just become godly, *we have to train ourselves to be godly.* In the same way that an athlete prepares himself/herself for a track meet through consistent and vigorous training, the Christian has to train himself to walk in a godly manner.

A godly person can be defined as one who has great respect for the Lord and this reverence for God is seen in their obedience to the word of God. We become godly by training our minds to think biblically and we develop this mindset by practicing two things;

1. Reading the word of God and uplifting literature; and

2. Training our minds to reject unprofitable information.

Reading the word of God is absolutely essential in order to train the mind to think in a biblical manner. It is also important for the Christian to continually expose his mind to science, philosophy, history, psychology and other edifying literature from various fields of study. While we cannot read everything, there are some really good books out there that we ought to devour. There are many outstanding Christian authors who have contributed greatly to the body of Christ through their work. It is essential that we read their material as such reading helps to train our minds to think biblically and positively. Reading edifying information also helps in forming a godly and informed worldview which will greatly help one to live in a godly manner.

As we immerse our minds in the word of God and edifying literature we will not only be more prepared to discern that which is unprofitable, but we will increasingly find unprofitable information repulsive. The Lord has a way of exposing the counterfeit nature of sin and making sin appear increasingly sinful to those who continually expose themselves to his word.

As we fill our minds with the word of God and godly literature we will be training ourselves to think and act in a godly manner. Let us forget that which is unedifying and hold on to that which is good.

Remember:

The mind must be trained to think in a godly manner.

Challenge:

1. Memorize Philippians 4:8.

"Finally brothers, whatever is true, whatever is noble, whatever is right, whatever is pure, whatever is lovely, whatever is admirable- if anything is excellent or praiseworthy- think about such things."

Philippians 4:8

2. Buy one book that can help you to think in a godly manner and read it through in a month or less. Share the information that you have learned with someone.

Prayer For Today

Heavenly Father, help me today to fill my mind with that which is godly and edifying. Strengthen me through the power of the Holy Spirit and help me to practice to think on that which is true, pure and praiseworthy. I renounce all unproductive and negative thoughts and I commit my mind to your holy word. Heavenly Father, give me the victory in my thoughts today. In Jesus' name I pray.

Amen.

PERSONAL REFLECTIONS

GOD'S WORD...MY WEAPON

Jesus answered, "It is written: 'Man does not live on bread alone, but on every word that comes from the mouth of God.'"

Mathew 4:4

"How can a young man keep his way pure? By living according to your word."

Psalm 119:9

One of the most amazing things about the word of God is that it can be used as a weapon. God's word is alive and powerful (Hebrews 4:12) and it can be used to demolish every stronghold that Satan and his horde of demonic forces could ever bring against us (2Corinthians 10:4). Satan would certainly want us to be shy and insecure about the power of the word of God and stay silent in the midst of spiritual warfare because he knows the damage that would be done to his kingdom if we declare the word of God.

God's word must be used and we use it by speaking it in the midst of situations, temptations and circumstances we encounter. Every time our Lord and Savior Jesus Christ was tempted He declared the word of God and stood firmly against the devil.

Let us consider three things our Lord did in order to stand in the day of temptation:

1. He memorized God's word;

2. He believed God's word;

3. He declared God's word.

Jesus was able to say, "It is written" each time he was tempted because the word of God was in his head. He had memorized the word of God. If we are going to walk in sexual purity, we must memorize the verses that deal with sexual sin so that in the day of temptation we can speak forth God's word boldly. The Spirit of God will use the spoken word to demolish the spiritual forces that are trying to make us yield to the temptation.

The second thought to keep in mind is that Jesus was able to declare the word of God in the face of temptation because He believed the word. What we practice is a true indicator of what we believe. Our belief system is being molded each and every day. When we immerse ourselves in God's word, we are literally training ourselves to believe the word of God above everything else. As we mature in our belief in God's word, we will use the word instead of other strategies. Some people will try taking cold showers to destroy their sexual urges but cold showers are useless in destroying the root of sexually immoral desires. Sexual immoral desires arise from within the heart (Mathew 15:19). It is the heart that needs to be changed. Our hearts are changed as we believe the word of God. 'Belief' or 'faith' matures in our lives as we immerse ourselves in God's word (Romans 10:17).

The third and final thing we learn from our Lord is that there is power in the spoken word of God. When God created the world, we are told in Genesis chapter 1, that God spoke in order to create. When God speaks, it is like no other. Mountains move when our God speaks (Mathew 21:21). The powerful fact is that God's word has that same power today. The Bible is God's word and, when it is declared, it has the power to do great things. Jesus knew the power of the word of God. He knew that when he declared the word of God in the face of the temptation he was defeating and destroying the forces of darkness. In the same way, when we as the children of God declare His powerful word, we are destroying the work of darkness in and over our lives. Let us therefore boldly declare God's word when we are tempted to sin sexually and experience the power of a victorious walk of purity.

Remember:

The word of God is a powerful weapon that must be used.

Challenge:

Memorize Romans 6:1-2 and Romans 6:12-14.

"What shall we say, then? Shall we go on sinning so that grace may increase? By no means! We died to sin; how can we live in it any longer?"

Romans 6:1-2

"Therefore do not let sin reign in your mortal body so that you obey its evil desires. Do not offer the parts of your body to sin, as instruments of wickedness, but rather offer yourselves to God, as those who have been brought from death to life; and offer the parts of your body to him as instruments of righteousness."

Romans 6:12-14

Prayer For Today

Almighty God, I thank You for Your word. Help me to use it today to come against all the fiery darts of the enemy. Thank You for giving me the authority through Jesus Christ to use Your word in the face of every temptation or test I go through. I commit myself to You and ask You to give me the victory today in all the temptations that will come my way. In Jesus' name I pray.

Amen.

PERSONAL REFLECTIONS

_____

_____

_____

_____

_____

_____

_____

_____

_____

_____

_____

_____

_____

_____

_____

_____

_____

_____

_____

_____

WATCH YOUR EYES

"If your right eye causes you to sin, gouge it out and throw it away. It is better for you to lose one part of your body than for your whole body to be thrown into hell."

Mathew 5:29

"I will set before my eyes no vile thing."

Psalm 101:3

"One evening David got up from his bed and walked around on the roof of the palace. From the roof he saw a woman bathing. The woman was very beautiful,"

2 Samuel 11:2

Sexual impurity is all around us. We certainly do not have to look too far to find some form of sexually explicit information. If we are watching television for example, we are very likely to see a sexually-oriented advertisement. Almost every music video has not just sexual content but the glorification of this type of content. Sadly, sexually immoral content is also on the roads, in the clothing stores, in the pharmacies and all over. It almost seems impossible to go through one day without seeing some form of sexually immoral content, unless, of course, we live as hermits. Fortunately, there is a way for us to live holy lives without being in isolation.

In order for us to walk in sexual purity, one of the things we have to learn is to guard our eyes. This is done by practicing to turn our attention away from impure images. Pictures have a way of making a greater impression on our minds than words. At one point or another, we have all heard the expression: "A picture is worth a thousand words". Pictures can be more easily replayed in our minds than statements and this means that in the absence of the actual picture we can imagine it and continue to 'feast our eyes' on it in the privacy of our minds. The more we think on the image, the more we allow it to make an indelible impression in our minds and it becomes very hard to forget.

In order to see the devastating consequences of impure imaginations, we can look at one of King David's failures. In 2 Samuel 11, we are told about the story of King David's adultery with Bathsheba. What is interesting is how King David ended up sinning against the Lord. He was on the roof of his house at a time when he was supposed to be at war and he happened to see a beautiful woman taking a bath. When he saw Bathsheba bathing he had a choice. He could either feast his eyes on the naked woman or he could turn his eyes away from her. Unfortunately, King David continued to feast his eyes on the lady and it led to his spiritual failure. David's failure was not that he saw Bathsheba bathing; his failure was that he chose to continue looking at her after he first happened to see her. His glance eventually turned into a libidinous leer.

Fortunately, King David repented of his act of adultery and never gave himself to such behavior again. He recognized the importance of guarding his eyes, so much so that he eventually wrote "I will set before my eyes no vile thing" (Psalm 101:3).

Today, let us practice to turn our eyes away from sexually impure images. We cannot always prevent ourselves from seeing sexual content but we can surely choose to turn our eyes away from sexual content that we happen to see.

Remember:

Turn your eyes away from impure images.

Challenge:

Memorize Job 31:1.

"I made a covenant with my eyes not to look lustfully at a girl."

Job 31:1

Throughout today turn your eyes away from sexually impure images. Tell a good Christian friend about your challenge for today and ask him/her to ask you how you did at the end of the day.

Prayer For Today

Heavenly Father, I commit my eyes to You today. There are many images which I will happen to see throughout the day and I ask You to give me the spiritual strength to turn my eyes away from all impure images. Today, I make a covenant with my eyes not to look at anyone in a lustful manner and I ask You to give me the victory today. In Jesus' name I pray.

Amen.

PERSONAL REFLECTIONS

RUN FOR YOUR LIFE !

"Flee from sexual immorality. All other sins a man commits are outside his body but he who sins sexually sins against his own body".

1 Corinthians 6:18

"She caught him by his cloak and said, "Come to bed with me!" But he left his cloak in her hand and ran out of the house."

Genesis 39:12

"But among you there must not be even a hint of sexual immorality"

Ephesians 5:3a

Sexual urges are extremely powerful. In many cases when drug addicts try to explain how they feel when they are high, they tend to make an analogy with a sexual feeling, in order to convey what they are experiencing in that moment. God is the author of sex and He did a very good job of creating our bodies in a way that we would surely enjoy this activity (of course, within the context of marriage).

In light of the fact that sexual desires are so powerful, it is important that we do not flirt with them. Some people believe that they can do all sorts of physical stuff such as fondling, kissing and caressing and that as long as they do not have sexual intercourse, they are fine. God's word however does not say that we should resist sexual intercourse, it says that we should run away from sexual sin (1 Corinthians 6:18). In other words, God expects us to move far away from all sexually impure activities. What we must realize is that sexual activity involves much more than sexual intercourse in and of itself. Sex involves cuddling, kissing, sexual touches, caressing and much more before sexual intercourse occurs. Sexual intercourse is a part of the sex act. God's word does not encourage us to abstain from sexual intercourse, it instructs us to run away from all sexual activity outside of the context of marriage. Ephesians 5:3 tells us that we should not have even a hint of sexual immorality in our lives.

There is at least one person in the word of God who teaches us that we should run from sexual sin. His name is Joseph. Joseph was a young handsome man who was repeatedly tempted to commit sexual sin with his boss' wife. (This story can be found in Genesis 39). Joseph literally ran from this lady. He did not try to resist her by staying in her presence. He used what energy he had to run away from her. He ran because he wanted to honor the Lord with his body. When faced with the temptation to commit sexual sin, Joseph responded by saying "How could I do such a wicked thing and sin against God?" Joseph was more interested in honoring God rather than giving in to his sexual urges. He saw sexual sin as a wicked thing in the eyes of God and he did not want to fail God in that way.

As people who want to walk in sexual purity, we cannot make up our own rules for sexual activity. Sexual feelings are very powerful and we must not flirt with them or remain in the atmosphere of those feelings. The only way out of sexual failure is to run far away from it. Sometimes our 'running' might include ending a relationship that is constantly causing us to compromise our sexual purity, or it might include getting rid of material that is encouraging us to fall. At other times, 'running' might include asking a trusted friend to keep us accountable during our day to day interactions with others.

Whatever the situation, we all can and must run away from sexual failure.

Remember:

You can run from sexual failure.

Challenge:

1) Are you in a sexually impure relationship? If you are, the challenge for today is to meet with a trusted Christian leader or friend who can counsel both of you towards a sexually pure walk. If you do not have a trusted Christian friend, then speak with your Pastor.

2) **Memorize 1 Corinthians 6:18**

"Flee from sexual immorality. All other sins a man commits are outside his body but he who sins sexually sins against his own body".

1 Corinthians 6:18

Prayer For Today

Heavenly Father, I commit my body to You today and dedicate myself to the pursuit of holiness. Help me to know the difference between that which is unholy and that which is holy and to give myself to holiness. Give me a heart that is sensitive to Your word and Your voice and when I am moving in a direction that is contrary to that which is holy speak to me Lord and give me the strength to listen and obey. I renounce all unholy behavior and offer the members of my body to You Lord. In Jesus' name I pray.

Amen.

PERSONAL REFLECTIONS

_____

_____

_____

_____

_____

_____

_____

_____

_____

_____

_____

_____

_____

_____

_____

_____

_____

TELL IT LIKE IT IS

"Therefore confess your sins to each other and pray for each other so that you may be healed".

James 5:16

"Then the man and his wife heard the sound of the Lord God as he was walking in the garden in the cool of the day, and they hid from the Lord God among the trees of the garden".

Genesis 3:8

Sometimes the most difficult thing to do is to admit that you did something wrong. For most people the number one reason they find it hard to confess their sins is because they are afraid of the consequences that could follow. Just imagine a husband having to confess to his wife that he was unfaithful to her. He would most likely be afraid of how she would respond to him. If he has children he would be very afraid of what his kids might think of him and if he is a leader in his church he might fear being rejected by the people of his congregation.

When we sin, our first tendency is to try to remove any evidence of our failure. Like Adam and Eve we hide ourselves hoping that somehow no one will know what we did. While sometimes we may be successful at concealing our sin, we are miserable failures when it comes to removing our guilt. Guilty feelings will always follow sin. Guilt makes us very uncomfortable and unhappy and the more we conceal our sin, the more guilt we experience. What then is the solution to this problem?

There is only one solution to the problem of guilt and that is confession. The very thing that we don't want to do, is the very thing that will release us from our guilt. Confession is a powerful tool that opens the door for real life-breathing freedom. When we don't confess our sins we experience spiritual bondage. This means that we lack the freedom to be who we really are. We become first class hypocrites who constantly put on a show before others by hiding the truth about ourselves as we display a lie.

The word of God tells us that if we confess our sins to others, we will be healed (James 5:16). This does not mean we should just speak to any and anybody about our business. We must find a trusted friend or godly leader and confess our faults to that person. While confessing our sins, we may feel very uncomfortable, but, as we speak about our failures we will experience God's healing and we will be free, truly free. Proverbs 28:13 says: "He who conceals his sins does not prosper, but whoever confesses and renounces them finds mercy".

Let us experience the healing power of God by confessing our sins today. It is better to be a little uncomfortable and experience total freedom than to appear comfortable and be heavily steeped in spiritual bondage.

Remember:

Confession brings true freedom

Challenge:

1) Find a trusted friend and confess your sexual struggles to that person. Ask them to pray for you and allow the Lord to free you from all forms of spiritual bondage.

2) Memorize James 5:16

"Therefore confess your sins to each other and pray for each other so that you may be healed".

James 5:16

Prayer For Today

Heavenly Father, I thank You for drawing near to me in the midst of my failures. Thank You for not leaving me to myself to be destroyed in guilt and shame. I am indeed so grateful that I can come to You and confess my failures and receive forgiveness from You. I understand the importance of also confessing my sins to others and I ask You to place someone in my life with whom I can be comfortable speaking with about my failures and struggles. As I confess to others, Lord, I thank You for freeing me from all my sin, guilt and shame. Dear Lord, strengthen my inner man and help me to walk uprightly. All these things I pray in the precious name of Jesus.

Amen.

PERSONAL REFLECTIONS

_____

_____

_____

_____

_____

_____

_____

_____

_____

_____

_____

_____

_____

_____

_____

_____

_____

IT'S TIME TO PRAY

"Watch and pray so that you will not fall into temptation…"
Mathew 26:41a

"Epaphras, who is one of you and a servant of Christ Jesus sends greetings. He is always wrestling in prayer for you, that you may stand firm in all the will of God, mature and fully assured."
Colossians 4:12

Prayer is an extremely potent weapon given to the body of Christ. While Jesus walked the face of this earth He was a man of prayer. The word of God tells us that at times Jesus prayed very early in the morning (Mark 1:35) and there were also times he would pray straight through the night (Luke 6:12).

On the night that Jesus was betrayed by one of his disciples he said to them "Watch and pray so that you will not fall into temptation". Jesus made it abundantly clear that prayer was absolutely necessary in order to stand in the day of temptation and not fall into sin. A prayer-less Christian will always be a spiritually weak one. In order for us to grow spiritually, we must practice the discipline of praying. I use the word 'discipline' because we are not naturally inclined to pray. The habit of praying must be cultivated and this takes discipline. As we continue in the discipline of prayer, we will find ourselves delighting in prayer.

Colossians 4:12 tells us three things that prayer will accomplish in our lives:

1. Prayer helps us to stand firm in all the will of God;

2. Prayer helps us to mature spiritually;

3. Prayer makes us fully assured.

Let us look at each of these points.

Prayer helps us to stand firm in all the will of God
We are always being tempted to abort the will of God. There are times when we feel discouraged, or we are filled with despair, and we think to ourselves that there is no way out of our situation. These feelings can sometimes lead us to doubt God's purpose in our lives and to doubt His word. Through prayer we are able to tear down the lies of Satan and stand firmly in the will of God, despite the circumstances we face. As we pray we will receive the spiritual fortitude we need to withstand all negative and demonic insinuations and we will be able to stand firmly in all the will of God.

Prayer helps us to mature
The more a Christian grows up in his faith, the less he/she will sin. As we spend time in prayer, our inner being will become increasingly stronger. This strength is what we need to stand in the day of temptation. What is really happening as we pray, is that we are becoming more and more like our Lord and Savior Jesus Christ. As we mature into his likeness through prayer, we become less attracted to sin.

Prayer makes us fully assured

We grow in confidence as we pray. This 'confidence' is not a self-sufficient confidence, it is confidence that you are in God's will. As we spend time in prayer, the Spirit of God will fill us with godly conviction, making us very much aware of what is right in the eyes of the Lord and provide us with the godly conviction to walk in the right path.

In light of these three attributes that will be formed in us through habitual prayer, let us call upon the name of the living God and receive the power we need to stand against sexual sin.

Remember:

It is through prayer that spiritual strength is received.

Challenge:

1) Commit to spending at least fifteen minutes in prayer today. You don't have to do it all at once. The habit of prayer is best developed by doing a little each day.

2) Memorize Colossians 4:12

"Epaphras, who is one of you and a servant of Christ Jesus sends greetings. He is always wrestling in prayer for you, that you may stand firm in all the will of God, mature and fully assured".

Colossians 4:12

Prayer For Today

Dear Lord, as You taught the disciples to pray, I ask You to teach me to pray. Let me know the sweetness of Your presence. Open my ears to hear Your voice and give me a heart that longs to be devoted to You. Even today, I ask You to reveal Yourself to me as I pray and when I fail to pray, I ask You to remind me, Lord, and give me the strength to call upon Your name. All these things I pray in Jesus' name.

Amen.

PERSONAL REFLECTIONS

DAY 12

OUR GOD FORGIVES

"If we confess our sins, he is faithful and just and will forgive us our sins and purify us from all unrighteousness".

1 John 1:9

Sometimes we experience failure after failure and we might be tempted to think that the Lord is tired of us or we might think that it makes no sense to repeatedly come to God about the same issues. There are many Christians who walk around with a heavy sense of guilt and self-condemnation because they think that somehow God has no interest in them or that he has grown weary with their repetitive sin and will not forgive them again. This type of negative thinking is due to a lack of understanding about the character of God.

Although we might experience our sin weighing heavily on our hearts, we must remember that the shed blood of Jesus is powerful and able to cleanse us from any and every sin. Satan's aim is always to diminish the power of the work of God and exalt our failures in such a way that it appears to us that nothing could ever wash away our sin-stained souls. 1 John 1:9 says: "If we confess our sins, he is faithful and just and will forgive us our sins and purify us from all unrighteousness". Jesus made it possible for us to be forgiven again and again when he died and shed His blood on the cross. This does not mean that God wants us to sin repeatedly, certainly not! What it means is that God so desperately wants us to be holy that he has made it possible for us to be repeatedly cleansed from our sins. God's desire for us to be holy is so great that when he sees our sin, His first desire is to clean us up so that we can be purified from all unrighteousness. Let us not forget this; Jesus died on the cross so that we might be forgiven of our sins and become holy and acceptable to God. Therefore when we fail God let us not think for a moment that he wants us to remain in a guilty and dirty state. No, God wants to clean us up; He is more than willing to forgive us again and again and to cleanse us again and again and again because of His desire for us to be without blemish or stain. Our God cleans us up.

Let us therefore confess our sins to the Lord and allow him to purify us from all unrighteousness.

Remember:

God, in his faithfulness, forgives us again and again.

Challenge:

Memorize Psalm 103:8-10

"The Lord is compassionate and gracious, slow to anger, abounding in love. He will not always accuse, nor will he harbor his anger forever; he does not treat us as our sins deserve or repay us according to our iniquities."

Psalm 103:8-10

As you go through this day, meditate on Psalm 103. Keep the character of God at the forefront of your mind and be encouraged in your journey towards sexual purity.

Prayer For Today

Heavenly Father, I praise You for being forgiving, compassionate and gracious to me. I Thank You for being slow to anger towards me and also for overwhelming me in Your love. I thank You for not treating me as my sins deserve or repaying me in accordance with my folly. Thank You for the great God You are, who purifies me when I confess my sins to You. I thank You for Your great mercy towards me and Your faithfulness in my life. Thank You dear Lord for who You are in Jesus' name I pray.

Amen.

PERSONAL REFLECTIONS

DAY 13

GOD'S WILL REVEALED

"It is God's will that you should be sanctified: that you should avoid sexual immorality; that each of you should learn to control his own body in a way that is holy and honorable, not in passionate lust like the heathen, who do not know God"

1 Thessalonians 4:3-5

"But just as he who called you is holy, so be holy in all you do; for it is written: "Be holy, because I am holy."

1 Peter 1:15-16

As we spend time in the word of God, we become better at being able to discern the will of God. There are some aspects of His will however, that He does not want us to discern or figure out eventually; He wants us to know those aspects now and He has clearly spelled them out for us in His word. A passage that unequivocally communicates the specific will of God for all his people is found in 1 Thessalonians 4: 3-5 which says: "It is God's will that you should be sanctified: that you should avoid sexual immorality; that each of you should learn to control his own body in a way that is holy and honorable, not in passionate lust like the heathen, who do not know God".

Let us consider three thoughts from this passage.

1) It is God's will that you should be sanctified

The first requirement that God demands of us is to be sanctified people. The word 'sanctified' is translated from the Greek word 'hagiasmos' which speaks to the process whereby one is progressively advancing towards the holy character of Jesus Christ. God therefore wants all of His people to mature in holiness. Although we were made holy when we repented of our sins and accepted Jesus as the Lord of our lives, we are expected to live out this holiness on a day to day basis. In order for a lifestyle of holiness to be developed, we must have a daily aim to walk in obedience to the word of God. We will never accidentally walk in obedience to God's word. Our obedience will only occur if we make up our minds to obey the Lord each day.

2) It is God's will that you should avoid sexual immorality

The second thing that God makes clear to us is that He wants us to avoid sexually immoral behavior. It is important to remember that sexually immoral behavior includes sexual intercourse but is not confined to it. Too many times we are creating our own rules about sexual behavior and many of us are guilty of trying to see how close we can get to 'sin' without 'actually sinning'. The Lord wants us to AVOID sexual immorality. Avoiding sexual sin involves taking all the necessary practical steps to make sure that there is no chance of any sexual misconduct.

3) It is God's will that you should learn to control your own body in a way that is holy and honorable

Self-control is a fruit of the Spirit. As a Christian grows more and more into the image and likeness of Christ, he will increasingly display the godly attitude of self-control. In order for self-control to be birthed in our lives we have to practice obeying the word of God in the midst of temptation.

We cannot allow ourselves to do as we please, for a self-pleasing lifestyle is totally contrary to the spirit of Christlikeness. We have to learn to control our bodies in a holy and honorable manner. This 'learning' involves being sensitive to those situations where we are most likely to be impure and avoiding them. It also involves being quick to recognize when unproductive and worthless thoughts enter our minds as well as choosing not to dwell on those impure thoughts but instead, replacing them with biblical ones.

The word of God makes it clear to us that those who are involved in immoral behavior are those who do not *know* God (1 Thessalonians 4:5), but since we know the Lord, let us behave in a holy and honorable manner.

Remember:

It is God's will for me to be sanctified.

Challenge:

Memorize 1 Thessalonians 4:3-5.

"It is God's will that you should be sanctified: that you should avoid sexual immorality; that each of you should learn to control his own body in a way that is holy and honorable, not in passionate lust like the heathen, who do not know God".

Prayer For Today

Dear Lord, You have called me to be holy and that is what I want to be. I ask You to fill my heart with a passion for holiness. Help me to be self-controlled and to learn to conduct myself in a manner that is honorable to Your name. Irrespective of what comes my way today, give me the strength to honor You in my attitude. All these things I pray in Jesus' name.

Amen.

PERSONAL REFLECTIONS

_____

_____

_____

_____

_____

_____

_____

_____

_____

_____

_____

_____

_____

_____

_____

_____

_____

ARE WE ON THE SAME PAGE?

"Do not be yoked together with unbelievers. For what do righteousness and wickedness have in common? Or what fellowship can light have with darkness? What harmony is there between Christ and Belial? What does a believer have in common with an unbeliever?"

2 Corinthians 6:14-15

In my time in ministry, I have observed that some Christians end up in a sexually immoral lifestyle after first entering a relationship with an unbeliever. The devastating consequences of this type of relationship tend to be rather painful. Usually, the Christian ends up in a backslidden state, separates himself from the body of Christ and eventually loses his/her interest in the things of God.

The Christian is given a direct instruction about relationships with non-Christians. He is commanded not to enter into that type of relationship. The word of God goes even further to emphasize the futility of such an interaction. God's word tells us that there will be no common ground between the Christian and the non-Christian. If a relationship is going to work, both parties must have the same worldview. The worldview of a non-Christian is not a Christ-centered one and therefore he (or she) will not live his life as one with Jesus as Lord. The non-Christian might be a nice person with many wonderful attributes, but the core of his inner being will be filled with unrepentant sin. A born-again believer will never share common ground with a non-Christian. In order for an unequally yoked relationship to work the Christian will have to deny Christ as his Lord. What would be the sense of a Christian doing that? He/she would be rejecting the author of life and going back into a life of sin.

In the same way that righteousness has no commonality with wickedness so the Christian will find that there is no common ground with the non-Christian. And just as fellowship can never occur between light and darkness, so the Christian will find that there can be no true fellowship between himself and a non-Christian. Likewise, just as harmony will never occur between Christ and Belial, the Christian will find no harmony in a union with a non-Christian.

The desire to walk in sexual purity is a God-given desire. Let us not destroy our God given desires by being unequally yoked.

Remember:

There can be no fellowship between light and darkness

Challenge:

Memorize 2 Corinthians 6:14-15

"Do not be yoked together with unbelievers. For what do righteousness and wickedness have in common? Or what fellowship can light have with darkness? What harmony is there between Christ and Belial? What does a believer have in common with an unbeliever?"

2 Corinthians 6:14-15

Prayer For Today

Heavenly Father, there are times I am drawn away from being faithful to You because of my attraction to those who are not believers. I ask You Lord, to help me to wait on You to provide someone for me and not to run ahead in my own direction. Give me a heart that wants what You want for me and help me to learn to trust You in everything. All these things I pray in the name of Jesus.

Amen.

PERSONAL REFLECTIONS

THE BLESSED MAN

"Blessed is the man who perseveres under trial, because when he has stood the test, he will receive the crown of life that God has promised to those who love him"

James 1:12

It is a very good thing to encourage yourself or be encouraged by someone after failing in the day of temptation, but it is indeed a better thing to have never failed in the first place. It is important that we understand, as the people of God that it is possible to walk through temptation and not be defeated. The word of God is filled with many examples of individuals who were faithful to the Lord while they were tempted. Enoch was one such person. He walked with God in a decadent world and did not give in to the temptation to compromise his purity before the Lord. As a result of his faithful walk, the Lord kept him from experiencing death (Genesis 5:22-24). Another example is Noah. Noah was basically a minister whose ministry, although very effective only impacted about eight people and those eight came from his own family. Instead of getting discouraged and cursing God or giving up on the call of God, he persevered and remained faithful to the Lord and God used him to preserve the world from being destroyed by a flood. The final example I will use is Daniel, an Israelite who was in captivity in Babylon. While there, he purposed in his heart that he was not going to dishonor the Lord by defiling himself with the king's food (Daniel 1:8). Daniel risked his life in order to honor the Lord while remaining faithful to the Israelite law. God saw his purity of heart and preserved his life from being snuffed out by the Babylonians. All three of these biblical stalwarts were tempted but passed the test in the day of temptation.

It is essential for us to be cognizant of the fact that we do not have to fall into sin when we are tempted. We should therefore not see temptation as an opportunity for us to sin. Instead, we should view every temptation as a test which provides us with the opportunity to strengthen our resolve to honor the Lord. When we practice standing in the day of temptation, we become spiritually stronger and it actually becomes easier for us to honor the Lord. On the other hand, when we fail in the temptation, we become spiritually weaker and it becomes easier for us to give in to sinful behavior.

IF we stand in the day of temptation, the word of God tells us that we will be rewarded with the crown of life (James 1:12). Let us therefore not make it a habit to fail the Lord in our time of testing. Let us make up our minds, irrespective of how powerful the temptation comes, to stand as the people of God.

Remember:

I can stand in the test

Challenge:

Memorize James 1:12.

"Blessed is the man who perseveres under trial, because when he has stood the test, he will receive the crown of life that God has promised to those who love him."

James 1:12

Prayer For Today

Heavenly Father, help me to stand today in the face of all temptations that will come my way. Give me a heart that is deeply attracted to honoring You. Today I set my mind on that which is holy and renounce all that which is unholy and I ask You Lord to give me the strength I need today to bring glory to Your name through all my actions. All these things I pray in the name of Jesus.

Amen.

PERSONAL REFLECTIONS

DON'T BLAME GOD

"When tempted, no one should say, "God is tempting me." For God cannot be tempted by evil, nor does he tempt anyone."
James 1:13

I once had a conversation with a young lady who got pregnant outside of the context of marriage. While this situation does not seem to be much of a big deal by the standards of the society today, the individual was exposed to much public ridicule because of a particular position she held at the time. While speaking with her she said, "I don't know why the Lord has allowed this to happen to me at this time." In the midst of her situation she was blaming God for her failure and not taking responsibility for her own choices. I had to remind her that God was the one convicting her before she ended up sinning in order to help her not to experience the embarrassing consequences she was now facing.

Some people are very quick to blame God when they fall in the day of temptation, but God is not the source of our spiritual failures (James 1:13). God has absolutely nothing to do with evil. He has no evil passion to be gratified as He is the epitome of holiness. He has no evil desire for power, for He is the Almighty God. In Him, there is no evil desire for wealth, for He is the creator of all that is and furthermore, all that is or can be is already His. He certainly has no want of happiness, as all joy and happiness is found in Him. The word of God makes it abundantly clear that God is good (Psalm 107:1) and all that can ever come from a good God is good.

The question then, is: "How are we tempted?" The answer is found in James 1:14. We are told that all temptations come as a result of our own desires. It is our own desire for sexual immorality that causes us to be tempted to commit sexual sin. At the root of sexual sin therefore is a self-centered desire. As long as what we want is more important to us than what God wants for us, we will always please ourselves instead of Him. Pleasing God should be our only desire. Every time we sin, we have allowed our desire to satisfy self to supersede our desire to please God. Selfishness must therefore be crucified daily. We must quickly recognize that every temptation has, at the root of it, the forceful suggestion that one should live for himself. We are not here to please ourselves, we are the people of God and it is our innermost desire to live for the Lord and not ourselves. Let us go through today renouncing selfishness and let us focus our hearts on pleasing the living God.

Remember:

There is no need to blame God

Challenge:

Memorize James 1:13.

"When tempted, no one should say, "God is tempting me." For God cannot be tempted by evil, nor does he tempt anyone".

Prayer For Today

Heavenly Father, I confess to You that there are times I blame others for my own sinful failures. Help me to take responsibility for my sins and not get in the habit of trying to excuse myself. As I go through this day, I ask You to help me not to walk in a self-gratifying manner. Help me to set my mind and heart on pleasing You in all my ways. All these things I pray in Jesus' name.

Amen.

PERSONAL REFLECTIONS

_____

_____

_____

_____

_____

_____

_____

_____

_____

_____

_____

_____

_____

_____

_____

_____

_____

_____

I DON'T WANT
MY DESIRES

"When tempted, no one should say, "God is tempting me." For God cannot be tempted by evil, nor does he tempt anyone; but each one is tempted when, by his own evil desire, he is dragged away and enticed. Then, after desire has conceived, it gives birth to sin; and sin when it is full-grown, gives birth to death."

James 1:13-15

As Christians, it is imperative that we never allow ourselves to want something so badly that we become mastered by our desires. The apostle James tells us that our desires have the potential to drag us away from the right path (James 1:14). This means that our desires can become so powerful that they can lead us in a destructive direction. God's word provides us with more than a few examples of individuals who were unfortunately dragged away from a sincere desire to honor the Lord. let us look at one of those examples and see the effects of sinful desires.

Samson

Samson is possibly the most celebrated judge in the book of Judges. He had what I call a perfect start. Firstly, he was born to godly parents; secondly, he didn't have to go through the trouble of finding out his God-given purpose, because the Lord had revealed it to his parents before he was even conceived; thirdly, his gifts were being used from a young age; and finally, he had a relationship with the Lord. If ever there was a man who had no reason to fail the Lord, it was Samson.

Samson, however, had a big issue - he lacked self-control. All the problems into which he found himself were as a result of his uncontrollable emotions. His lack of self-control consistently led him to the wrong kind of women. In Judges 14 and 16 we see Samson having some form of a relationship with three women, one of whom was a prostitute and the other two were not Israelites - he clearly had the habit of being in unequally yoked relationships. Although he knew the Lord and was well acquainted with the movement of the Spirit of God in his life, he was constantly allowing his fleshly desires to drag him away from the right path. It was not that he lacked the spiritual fortitude to withstand the temptation to sin; it was that he kept allowing his sinful desires to rule him.

Samson was repeatedly led by his desires to the point where he was eventually made into a slave by his enemies, the Philistines (Judges 16:21). That is exactly what our sinful desires want to do to us; they want to turn us into slaves. Sinful desires cause us to feel excited about doing the wrong thing, but their true aim is to bring us into slavery.

Thankfully, Samson did not have a disgraceful end. While he was enslaved, he cried out to God and repented of his sinful ways and the Lord used him mightily to destroy the Philistines (Judges 16:28-30). What we can learn from his life however, is that sinful desires drag us away from the right path and lead us into a destructive one. Let us learn from Samson's mistakes. Let us not allow our desires to drag us away from the right path. Let us call upon the name of the Lord and ask Him to create in us a clean heart and renew within us a steadfast spirit (Psalm 51:10).

Remember:

Sinful desires only want to enslave us.

Challenge:

Memorize James 1:13-15.

"When tempted, no one should say, "God is tempting me." For God cannot be tempted by evil, nor does he tempt anyone; but each one is tempted when, by his own evil desire, he is dragged away and enticed. Then, after desire has conceived, it gives birth to sin; and sin when it is full-grown, gives birth to death."

James 1:13-15

Prayer For Today

Dear Lord, in accordance with Your word I ask You to create in me a clean heart and renew a steadfast spirit within me. Help me not to allow sexual desires to drag me away from the holy path You have called me to. Give me the spiritual fortitude I need today to submit to You and to resist the devil. All these things I pray in Jesus' name.

Amen.

PERSONAL REFLECTIONS

_____

_____

_____

_____

_____

_____

_____

_____

_____

_____

_____

_____

_____

_____

_____

_____

_____

DAY 18

WATCH YOUR WORDS!

"May the words of my mouth and the meditation of my heart be pleasing in your sight, O Lord, my Rock and my Redeemer".
Psalm 19:14

"Do not let any unwholesome talk come out of your mouths, but only what is helpful for building others up according to their needs, that it may benefit those who listen."
Ephesians 4:29

We live in a world today that glorifies impure speech. It has become the norm for movies to be filled with obscene language, for musical artists to use foul words, and for even authors to produce books riddled with lewdness. It is almost impossible to go through one day and not be exposed to something filthy proceeding from somebody's mouth.

It is quite easy for us to put ourselves in sexually impure situations by not keeping a close watch on the types of words that proceed from our mouths. Especially in the context of a relationship, we have to be very careful to watch what we express to each other as our words can be used to create feelings of arousal and lead us down an impure path. Our conversation can be used to foster helpful and edifying thoughts or degrading and destructive ones.

A very powerful verse that instructs us on the kind of words that should proceed from our mouths is found in Ephesians 4:29. It says: "Do not let any unwholesome talk come out of your mouths, but only what is helpful for building others up according to their needs, that it may benefit those who listen". From this verse, let us consider three thoughts.

1) We have control over what proceeds from our mouth

We are first told that we ought not to allow any unwholesome talk to proceed from our mouth. What we must note from this command is that we have the choice of controlling what comes out of our mouths. Self-control is an essential fruit of the Spirit in the life of every believer. We must take great care to exercise this gift by not allowing ourselves to simply do or say as we please. In the midst of every situation we face we have the ability to control how we respond. We certainly cannot control what we go through all the time but we can control ourselves regardless of what we are going through. Let us practice to control our tongue and declare words that will edify those who are listening and not lead others into sexual sin.

2) Our words must be helpful for building up

The second thing to note from this verse is that our words must be able to build others up. In our interactions with people, our first desire should be to help others to mature into the image and likeness of Jesus Christ. We should always be encouraging and challenging each other to mature in the faith. When we begin to encourage sexually immoral content in our conversations, we are working against the aim of our Christian goal, which is Christ-like maturity.

3) Our words should benefit those who listen

Anyone who is listening to our conversation should find it beneficial to hear what we are saying. Our content therefore should be filled with information that strengthens and inspires others towards a godly direction.

Let us commit ourselves to speaking forth words that will lead others away from sexual impurity and inspire them towards the pursuit of godliness.

Remember:

Our words must edify those who listen

Challenge:

Memorize Ephesians 4:29.

"Do not let any unwholesome talk come out of your mouths, but only what is helpful for building others up according to their needs, that it may benefit those who listen".

Ephesians 4:29

Prayer For Today

Heavenly Father, may the words of my mouth and the meditation of my heart be pleasing in Your sight, O Lord, my Strength and my Redeemer (Psalm 19:14).

Amen.

PERSONAL REFLECTIONS

_____

_____

_____

_____

_____

_____

_____

_____

_____

_____

_____

_____

_____

_____

_____

_____

_____

_____

FEARING GOD

"To fear the Lord is to hate evil; I hate pride and arrogance, evil behavior and perverse speech."

Proverbs 8:13

Moses said to the people, "Do not be afraid. God has come to test you, so that the fear of God will be with you to keep you from sinning."

Exodus 20:20

I once saw a video in which an alligator trainer who, while performing for a live audience put his hand into the mouth of the large reptile. The alligator kept its mouth open and remained still. The trainer then proceeded to put his hand deeper and deeper into the throat of the animal. Suddenly the reptile suddenly clamped its mouth shut on the arm of the trainer and started doing death rolls, severely damaging the arm of the trainer. Obviously playing with alligators, is not a wise pastime, even for an expert trainer. Such animals should be appreciated from a distance.

I certainly would never dare to put even my fingernail much less my hand near the mouth of such a ferocious animal, because of a healthy fear that God has put inside me. When we think of the word 'fear', many times we assume it means that we are afraid of something or someone, but not all fear suggests that. To fear something can also mean to respect it. Let us call this type of fear, 'healthy fear'. The 'healthy' fear of something can be a protective mechanism that allows us to be preserved and not destroyed. If we lose our healthy fear, we will foolishly expose ourselves to imminent danger and plunge headlong into a destructive direction. Therefore when we fear putting our finger into the mouth of an alligator, for example, it is because we understand the danger that exists and we respect that danger in such a way that we protect ourselves by not doing such a thing.

As Christians, we must develop a healthy fear of God. The fear of God matures in our lives as we expose our minds to His word and as we learn to obey God in little things. When we sin against the Lord, our hearts become increasingly insensitive to Him and we become hardened towards the Lord and the things of God. However, as we obey the Lord, our hearts become soft and we become increasingly sensitive to the Lord and the thought of sinning against the Lord is anathema to us. It is only as we grow in the fear of God that we will find the idea of sinning against the Lord increasingly repulsive. (Exodus 20:20).

Remember:

The fear of God matures in our lives as we obey God in little things.

Challenge:

Memorize Proverbs 8:13.

"To fear the Lord is to hate evil; I hate pride and arrogance, evil behavior and perverse speech."

Proverbs 8:13

Prayer For Today

Heavenly Father, I ask You to teach me Your ways and give me the strength to walk in Your truth. Give me an undivided heart, that I may fear Your name (Psalm 86:11) and not sin against You. Protect me from stubbornly going in my own direction and cause me to continually surrender myself to You. All these things I pray in the name of Jesus.

Amen.

PERSONAL REFLECTIONS

IT'S TIME TO ADD

"For this very reason, make every effort to add to your faith goodness."

2 Peter 2:5

"Make every effort to live in peace with all men and to be holy; without holiness no one will see the Lord."

Hebrews 12:14

Walking in purity will never occur unless we are maturing in our relationship with the Lord. The Apostle Peter encourages us to mature in our faith in Christ by making every effort to add other attributes to our faith (2 Peter 2:5-7). There are actually seven qualities that the apostle tells us to keep adding to our faith, but we will only look at one of those qualities.

Faith in Christ is essential to a life of purity but it is only the beginning. To our faith we must add goodness (2 Peter 2:5). The word 'goodness' means virtue or moral excellence. The word of God is therefore encouraging us to increasingly mature in our morality. While the topic of moral excellence encompasses a lot, we will just focus on one little section of it for today's devotion- blamelessness.

To be blameless does not mean to be perfect; it means to be above reproach as a result of moral purity. This means that, as Christians we should live in such a way that no one is able to say anything bad about us as a result of a moral failure. The world is always looking for a reason to malign the name of Jesus and since they cannot find any fault in Him, the world constantly looks for faults in His servants. As Christians, we do not want to give the world an opportunity to speak evil of the Christian faith and so we must be careful to protect our testimony from being tarnished. We protect our testimony by living blamelessly.

Sexual sin in the life of the believer provides a huge opportunity for the world to despise and to speak evil of the Christian faith. Satan loves it when a Christian falls into sin, especially sexual sin. He loves to publicize the failure to the world and embarrass not just the Christian who has sinned, but also, he gets an opportunity to embarrass the Christian faith.

We must therefore not see temptation as merely a personal attack, but also recognize it as an attack on the body of Christ. The devil tries to tear down the body of Christ through the failures of individual members. Therefore, whenever we are tempted to sin, we should bear in mind that our adversary, the devil, is only trying to destroy the body of Christ through its individual members.

The devil is not satisfied when one Christian falls. He wants the failure of one Christian to be so great that he can use that one failure to tear down the whole body of Christ. Let us therefore walk before the Lord in a blameless manner and not give the devil an opportunity to use our lives as an example for evil.

Remember:

Let us not give the world an opportunity to speak evil of the Christian faith.

Challenge:

Memorize 1Timothy 4:12.

"Do not let anyone look down on you because you are young, but set an example for the believers in speech, in life, in love, in faith and in purity.

1Timothy 4:12

Prayer For Today

Heavenly Father, I ask You to help me to walk in a blameless manner today. Give me the strength I need today to set an example to others in my speech, my life, my faith and in my purity. All these things I pray in the name of Jesus.

Amen.

PERSONAL REFLECTIONS

IT'S ALL ABOUT HIM

"Do you not know that your body is a temple of the Holy Spirit, who is in you, whom you have received from God? You are not your own; you were bought at a price. Therefore honor God with your body."

1 Corinthians 6:19-20

Temptations entice us to do evil. The word 'enticed' is purposely used as it means to lead on by exciting hope or desire. What actually happens in every temptation, is that we are encouraged to go in a direction contrary to Scripture with a false but exciting hope that our evil desires will satisfy us.

All temptations are designed to satisfy self. We are never tempted to deny ourselves, but to please ourselves. At the root of every temptation therefore, is the forceful suggestion that self-satisfaction is all that matters. Think about it - the husband who is unfaithful to his wife, the child who disregards godly instruction and the student who gives himself to indolent behavior all have one thing in common and that is self-gratification.

Every aspect of the Christian faith clearly encourages a selfless life and denounces selfishness. God's word unequivocally declares that we do not belong to ourselves (1 Corinthians 6:19-20). Our aim should never be to please self but, instead, to please the Lord who lived a selfless life and unselfishly died on a cross so that we might be reconciled to God. We have received life and life abundantly because of the selfless life and death of Jesus. It is in light of His selflessness that we are expected to honor God with our body.

As we grow more and more to appreciate all that has been done for us as a result of the cross of Christ, we will find it increasingly desirable to continually surrender ourselves to the Lord. It is in this surrendering that we find true freedom from our sinful desires. Let us commit ourselves to pleasing God and not ourselves and allow the Spirit of God to keep us pure, blameless and faultless until the coming of our Lord Jesus Christ.

Remember:

It is in light of Christ's selflessness that we are expected to honor God with our body.

Challenge:

Memorize 1 Corinthians 6:19-20.

"Do you not know that your body is a temple of the Holy Spirit, who is in you, whom you have received from God? You are not your own; you were bought at a price. Therefore honor God with your body."

1 Corinthians 6:19-20

Prayer For Today

Dear Lord, I thank You for shedding Your blood on a cross for me and giving me Your precious Holy Spirit. I ask You to let the message of the cross of Christ continually speak to me so that I may increasingly grow in the knowledge of Your unfailing love. Saturate me with a fervent desire for You and help me to honor You with my body and to glorify You all the days of my life. All these things I pray in the precious name of Jesus.

Amen.

PERSONAL REFLECTIONS

EPILOGUE

My prayer is that this little devotional will be used to help you to walk continually before your heavenly Father in sexual purity. As you have come to the end of this journey, I hope that you have been motivated, inspired and energized to fight for your purity. Never lose your zeal for holiness and do not allow failure to cause you to give up on your God-given desire to walk in purity. In your continued pursuit to walk before the Lord in holiness, I will leave you with a verse that has encouraged me countless times in my own journey:

"If we confess our sins, he is faithful and just and will forgive us our sins and purify us from all unrighteousness." (1 John 1:9)

May God richly bless you and use you to help many others to begin their own journey towards sexual purity.

ABOUT THE AUTHOR

Pastor Deon Omar (D. O.) Thomas

D. O. Thomas is the founder and Senior Pastor of The King's Sanctuary in Kingston, Jamaica and has been in Christian Ministry for over 16 years. As a pastor, teacher and accomplished musician, D. O. (as he is affectionately known) seeks to help people pursue Christ-likeness through teaching the Word of God and helping individuals apply it to their daily lives. He firmly believes that everyone has a God-given gift that should be developed and used in order to fulfill the purpose of God for their life.

Pastor Thomas has ministered as a speaker both locally and internationally challenging his hearers to find and execute their God-given purpose. Apart from church congregations, his audiences have included students at both the secondary and tertiary levels, staff of corporate entities, inmates at drug/rehabilitation centers, and young adults at youth organizations/conferences. In some instances, he served as the keynote speaker.

Pastor Deon is married to Joanna Elizabeth and they were recently blessed with an infant daughter, Amia Mercedes.

14301251R00061

Made in the USA
San Bernardino, CA
22 August 2014